The **1930s**
Britain in Pictures

The 1930s
Britain in Pictures

PA Photos

AMMONITE
PRESS

First Published 2008 by
Ammonite Press
an imprint of AE Publications Ltd,
166 High Street, Lewes, East Sussex BN7 1XU

Text copyright Ammonite Press
Images copyright PA Photos
Copyright in the work Ammonite Press

ISBN 978-1-906672-09-6

British Cataloguing in Publication Data. A catalogue
record of this book is available from the British Library.

Series Editor: Paul Richardson
Editor: Neil Dunnicliffe
Picture research: PA Photos
Design: Gravemaker + Scott

Colour reproduction by GMC Reprographics
Printed by Colorprint, China

Page 2: A penny-farthing
race at Herne Hill.
1st July, 1932

Page 5: The then-Duke
and Duchess of York in a
carriage along The Mall
leaving for Westminister
Abbey, for the Coronation
ceremony, after which they
became King George VI and
Queen Elizabeth.
12th May, 1937

Page 6: Troops leave
England for France.
10th October, 1939

Introduction

The archives of PA Photos yield a unique insight into Britain's recent past. Thanks to the science of photography we can view the 20th Century more accurately than any that came before, but it is thanks to news photography, and in particular the great news agency that is The Press Association, that we are able now to witness the events that made up life in Britain, not so long ago.

It is easy, looking back, to imagine a past neatly partitioned into clearly defined periods and dominated by landmarks: wars, political upheaval and economic trends. But the archive tells a different story: alongside the major events that constitute formal history are found the smaller things that had equal – if not greater – significance for ordinary people at the time. And while the photographers were working for that moment's news rather than posterity, the camera is an undiscriminating eye that records everything in its view: to modern eyes it is often the backgrounds of these pictures, not their intended subjects, that provide the greatest fascination.

The years between 1st January, 1930 and 31st December, 1939 saw the country at its most unstable. Britain's pre-Great War economic strength had been derived largely from its Empire, and post-war conditions were very different. Rapid industrial growth during the 1920s had been achieved through borrowing, leaving the economy over-extended and exposed when the Wall Street Crash sent shock waves across the developed world in 1929. Britain's exports halved, unemployment soared to over 20%, wage cuts were commonplace and the Depression took hold. The very real hardship that resulted – exacerbated by the hated Means Test – led to a profound deepening of social and political divisions, demonstrated by mass protests such as the Jarrow Hunger March. Three million Britons emigrated in search of a better life abroad and Fascism, overwhelming in Germany and Spain, gained a hold in Britain with Sir Oswald Mosley's British Union of Fascists. Even the monarchy faltered when Edward VIII abdicated at the end of 1936.

Yet at the end of this chaotic decade, the British people were able to unite and face the terrible prospect of a Second World War with seeming ease. Far from being the divided and weakened society suggested by the chaos and hardship of preceding years, Britain's domestic strength was to be its salvation during the conflict that followed. Although unanticipated, the new King, George VI, and his likeable family captured the hearts of the people and a leader who might have been born for the moment – Winston Churchill – emerged from the shadows to inspire the nation.

But it is in the faces of ordinary people of the time, pictured here getting on with their lives despite the political, social and economic tumult around them, that can be found an explanation for their readiness to march into a new war, a new decade – in many ways, a new world.

A man wearing Oxford bags,
a loose-fitting, baggy form
of trousers favoured by
members of the University
of Oxford, especially
undergraduates.
1930

Despatch Manager Walter
Cattermole with the
Press Association news
messenger boys outside the
PA building in Fleet Street,
London.
1930

A policeman halts the traffic
for a group of young ladies
wearing the latest in 'beach
pyjamas'.
1930

John Logie Baird with his 'Noctovisor', a machine for seeing through fog, in the grounds of his home at Box Hill.
1930

Already a qualified pilot,
Amy Johnson became the
first woman to gain an Air
Ministry Ground Engineer's
licence at the London
Aeroplane Club.
10th January, 1930

Lord and Lady Melchett
at Waterloo Station in
London, before leaving
for South Africa. Lord
Melchett is a leading figure
in the campaign for Empire
Economic Unity.
10th January, 1930

Norman Hartnell, the
famous young English dress
designer, describing his
models while being filmed
for Movitone News.
28th January, 1930

Facing page: Royal Navy
battleships steaming in line.
17th January, 1930

Kay Petre in her Bugatti
at Brooklands.
16th March, 1930

This picture, taken in a London public house, shows two men playing darts – the working-man's game that has become almost a national pastime. The picture shows the players putting the flights in their brass darts before the game.

17th March, 1930

Thousands of Arsenal fans pack the streets outside Islington Town Hall to greet the FA Cup winners as they make their way to a civic reception held in their honour.
28th April, 1930

HRH Queen Mary (L) with
some of the children from
the nursery school attached
to the Rachel McMillan
Training College in Deptford.
1st May, 1930

Miss Mary Turner, the 18 year old cricketer whose hurricane scoring has caused a sensation, is regarded as the best girl bat in the country. The picture shows Miss Turner during practice in the garden of her Surrey home.
11th May, 1930

The Epsom Derby.
12th May, 1930

Alec Jackson, Huddersfield
and Scottish international,
making a gramophone
record in London.
14th May, 1930

The new traffic signalling
device at Ludgate Circus.
19th May, 1930

The hunt moves off along
a road.
1 June, 1930

Cars parked on the banking
at Brooklands race track.
4th June, 1930

George Lott practising
at Wimbledon.
12th June, 1930

Ascot during the Gold Cup.
June, 1930

France's R Lacoste drives from the fourth tee, in the match between France and England at the Worplesdon Golf Club, Surrey.
22nd June, 1930

Flying boats, from Calshot
water aerodrome, at the
Hendon RAF pageant.
28th June, 1930

'Bosworth' leads the field
giving trainer, Lord Derby,
his first Gold Cup win at
Ascot.
30th June, 1930

London Transport trolley buses pulling out of Hounslow bus depot.
1st July, 1930

Factory girls and their
foreman.
1st July, 1930

Roland Harper (second R)
is pushed hard as he races
to victory in the 120 yards
hurdles final.
1st July, 1930

The Alfa Romeo of George
Eyston and his co-driver R
C Stewart is attended to by
mechanics before a record
attempt.
18th July, 1930

Madame Pavlova,
the famous dancer,
photographed in the grounds
of her home at Hampstead,
London.
21st July, 1930

The R101 at the mooring mast at Cardington before making a trial flight following extensive modifications, carried out during the summer after the airship's early trials in 1929 and the spring of 1930.
1st October, 1930

The Old Vic Theatre on
Waterloo Road, South
London.
1st October, 1930

The 500 mile race at Brooklands was won by S C Davis and the Earl of March in an Austin car. They won by 10 miles at an average speed of 83 mph. Here the winning car passes the post.
5th October, 1930

Motor racing at Brooklands.
16th October, 1930

Everton's Bill 'Dixie' Dean (L)
directs a header goalwards.
20th October, 1930

A portion of the vast crowd round the Mansion House during the two minute silence to commemorate the end of the First World War.
11th November, 1930

Middleweight Champion of
Europe Len Harvey, wearing
the Lonsdale Belt.
1931

Women's archery.
1931

Malcolm Campbell
(second L) and his team
with the Napier-Campbell
Bluebird, minus its
bodywork.
12th January, 1931

Malcolm Campbell, seated in
his 7.5HP Austin on Daytona
Beach, just prior to breaking
the world speed record for
'baby' cars.
10th February, 1931

Lord Beauchamp (L) and Sir
H Samuel in Central London.
22nd March, 1931

West Bromwich Albion
captain Tommy Glidden
(C) introduces the Duke of
Gloucester (third L) to his
team mates before the FA
Cup final.
25th April, 1931

Children in Hastings perform
sunbathing exercises.
1st May, 1931

The Duchess of York talking to a nurse at Harrow Hospital.
7th May, 1931

The parade of athletes
before the enormous crowd
which gathered to watch the
British Games.
25th May, 1931

The Prince of Wales leaving one of the Haig Homes for ex-servicemen at Morden, Surrey, after the official opening.
29th May, 1931

Princess Elizabeth visits
the Royal Tournament at
Olympia.
5th June, 1931

Queen Mary, Princess
Elizabeth and the Duchess
of York, on the way to the
Trooping of the Colour.
6th June, 1931

(L-R) Syd Edmonds and
Phil Bishop, High Beach
Speedway.
10th June, 1931

Fashion at Royal Ascot.
16th June, 1931

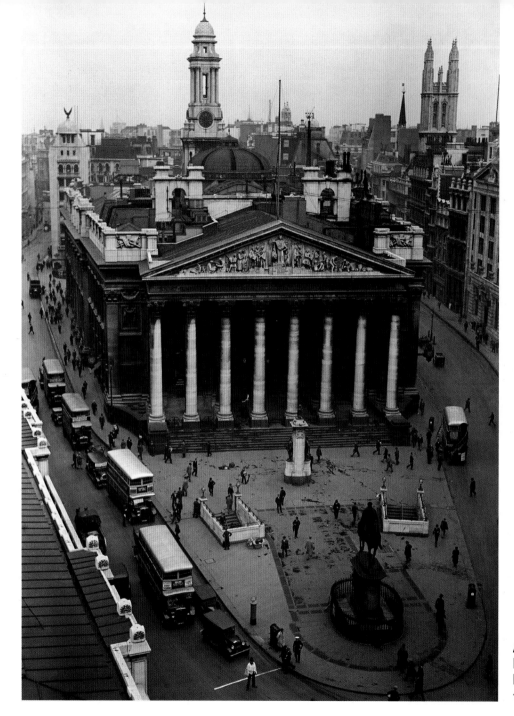

An aerial view of the Royal
Exchange in the City of
London.
18th June, 1931

Bobby Jones, golfer.
28th June, 1931

Street buskers broadcast
from the BBC.
29th June, 1931

Big Ben trying out its new floodlights for the Triennial International Illumination Congress which takes place in London.
21st July, 1931

Princess Elizabeth (C) and
her sister Princess Margaret
leaving Piccadilly, in London,
with their nanny in their
horse-drawn carriage.
22nd July, 1931

Leon Cushman in his record-
breaking supercharged Austin.
12th August, 1931

Squadron Leader Orlebar
about to start out for the
successful trial flight of
Britain's new Supermarine
Seaplane. This aircraft won
the Schneider Trophy at an
average speed of 340.8mph
and its designer, Reginald
Mitchell, went on to design
the legendary Supermarine
Spitfire.
13th August, 1931

A view of the newly-built
BBC Broadcasting House
in a wet central London.
13th August, 1931

A farm worker operates
a horse-drawn reaper-
binder during the harvest at
Teignmouth, South Devon.
14th August, 1931

An airship flying over
St Paul's Cathedral.
18th August, 1931

Flag making in a factory on
the Old Kent Road, London.
28th September, 1931

Port of London Authority
employees display some
leopard skins.
28th September, 1931

No. 10, Hyde Park Place, near Marble Arch. This tiny house, said to have been built for a lady's maid, consists of a front door and one room.
5th October, 1931

Children on rocking horses.
21st October, 1931

Canning Town children
having soup.
25th November, 1931

Facing page: Charles
Kingsford-Smith arriving
in the Southern Star at
Croydon with Christmas mail
from Australia.
16th December, 1931

Cooks at the ovens of the
Constitutional Club, London.
1st March, 1932

Facing page: A London
bus in the fog.
1st March, 1932

Manchester City goalkeeper
Len Langford (C) pushes
the ball away from Arsenal's
David Jack (second R) in the
FA Cup semi final.
12th March, 1932

A teleprinter being demonstrated at the annual British Industry Fair.
14th March, 1932

Scotland secure the ball as
England players press for
another try during the rugby
Five Nations Championship.
19th March, 1932

Scottish entertainer
Sir Harry Lauder on
a weighing machine.
18th April, 1932

Sir Malcolm Campbell's
Bluebird car, holder of the
World Land Speed Record,
at Brooklands.
20th April, 1932

Fifteen-year-old Elizabeth Hacking, who was the winner of the obstacle race at the Francis Holland, Graham Street, London school sports held at Battersea Park, London. The competitors had to balance a book on their heads and hold a skipping rope in one hand.
22nd April, 1932

George Bernard Shaw
arriving for the opening of
the Stratford Shakespeare
Memorial Theatre.
23rd April, 1932

Folk dancing in the streets
of Stratford-upon-Avon, after
the Prince of Wales opened
the new Shakespeare
Memorial Theatre.
23rd April, 1932

Aerial view of the action at
Wembley Stadium during
the FA Cup Final between
Arsenal and Newcastle
United.
23rd April, 1932

Debutantes being coached by Miss Josephine Bradley, the dance and deportment teacher, for forthcoming presentations at Buckingham Palace. The correct use of the fan will be much in favour this season.
28th April, 1932

Tazio Nuvolari in a Bugatti
at Brooklands.
1st May, 1932

A young lady at Halliford taking her canaries whilst moving to other quarters during the floods in London.
4th May, 1932

The London Olympiades Athletic Club held their first championship meeting of the season at Battersea Park, London. The picture shows Miss L Dawcett putting the shot.

14th May, 1932

Miss Eva Coleman, who intends to attempt to swim the Channel this summer, is using the Hyde Park Lido as a training ground. Picture shows Miss Coleman about to take the plunge.
19th May, 1932

General Freyberg, VC, chatting with CSM 'Joe' Bent. As a drummer with the 1st Bn, East Lancashire Regiment, Bent was awarded the Victoria Cross for his bravery during the First Battle of Ypres in 1914, when he rescued a wounded man under heavy German fire.

28th May, 1932

Facing page: Princess Elizabeth walking bareheaded through the rain.

27th May, 1932

Brooklands lap record holder
Sir Henry Birkin sits in his
Blower Bentley and talks
shop with Mrs Elsie Wisdom.
1st June, 1932

Miss Margaret Whigham and
Miss Holloway, fashionably
dressed to attend Ascot races.
14th June, 1932

The scoreboard at the County Ground, Leyton, tells the story after Yorkshire's Percy Holmes and Herbert Sutcliffe combined for a record first-class first wicket partnership of 555 against Essex.

16th June, 1932

(L-R) Brian Lewis, John Cobb, Tim Rose-Richards and A O Saunder Davis at Brooklands.
20th June, 1932

Kitty Brunell tunes up
her car's engine.
28th June, 1932

King George V welcomed home the Royal Welsh Fusiliers at Buckingham Palace, London, after they had been abroad for 18 years. Here the band of the Royal Welsh and their regimental goat march out of one of the Palace gates.
5th July, 1932

Karl Sander, a former German circus performer, demonstrates his novel way of advertising as he rides beside a bus in Streatham in south London.
9th August, 1932

The scene at the open air
baths at Kennington Park,
where south Londoners were
able to find relief from the
heat wave.
10th August, 1932

Two farm workers cut barley
using a horse-drawn reaper-
binder at St. Columb Minor,
near Newquay, Cornwall.
15th August, 1932

Youthful Thames anglers
taking part in a competition
arranged by the Chertsey
Angling Society.
27th August, 1932

Miss Betty Nuthall making
purchases at Covent Garden
Market in London.
6th October, 1932

Chelsea's George Mills (second L) tries to force his way through the Middlesbrough defence.
8th October, 1932

The herring catch being
landed on the Norfolk coast
of England. Newly arrived
drifters with their catch
alongside a Yarmouth wharf.
12th October, 1932

Hunger Marchers from Norfolk halt by the wayside at Brentford. They were demonstrating against the abolition of the Means Test and Anomalies Act and cuts in social services, and the 10% unemployment benefit cuts.

25th October, 1932

The Hunger Marchers'
demonstration at Marble
Arch, London.
27th October, 1932

The Nore Lightship
in dry dock.
1st November, 1932

Violinist Yehudi Menuhin
handing over an HMV record
to Sir Thomas Beecham at
Grosvenor House. On the
left is Sir Edward Elgar.
19th November, 1932

Facing page: Artist Stanley
Spencer at work on one of
his resurrection paintings for
the oratory in the village of
Burghclere, Hampshire.
8th December, 1932

Comedy artists Nervo, Knox and Eddie Gray, part of the Crazy Gang, in their sketch 'Fun at a petrol station'.
22nd December, 1932

Sir Malcolm Campbell
with his new 'Bluebird'.
1933

Two year old Princess
Margaret (seated) with her
sister Princess Elizabeth,
aged seven.
1933

A group of women display
some of the fashions for
1933 on their way to a
society wedding in London.
1933

In a BBC recording studio,
Christopher Stone, wearing
a dinner jacket, bids listeners
'Good Evening'.
1933

A gun team wearing gas
masks during fleet exercises
on board the HMS 'Versatile'.
1933

Ennis Hylton, at a rehearsal
for the Jack Hylton Band.
5th January, 1933

Men at work in precarious positions during the cleaning of Justice over the Old Bailey.
6th January, 1933

Crowds lining up for trams
during the bus strike.
23rd January, 1933

A section of the huge demonstration procession against the Government's unemployment policy, passing along the Embankment.

5th February, 1933

The Duke of York shakes
hands with the England
players before the England
v Ireland rugby match
during the Five Nations
Championship.
11th February, 1933

Tilting tests for new
London General Omnibus
Company buses.
10th March, 1933

The Post Master General
inspecting the first team of
boys with their motorcycles
at the G.P.O Yard.
13th March, 1933

Cecil Leitch (R) in play.
7th April, 1933

World land speed record
holder Malcolm Campbell
drives his record-breaking
'Bluebird' around
Brooklands.
17th April, 1933

Everton's Bill 'Dixie' Dean
holds up the FA Cup as the
team emerge onto Lime
Street, Liverpool.
1st May, 1933

Lizzie Sanger and Polly
Beecham (R), Piccadilly
flower sellers.
12th May, 1933

The Duchess of York (C) and her two daughters, Princess Elizabeth (second R) and Princess Margaret (R), at a disabled soldiers' sale of work.
16th May, 1933

Dame Ethel Locke-King (R),
owner of the Brooklands
track and wife of its founder,
Hugh Fortescue Locke-King.
23rd May, 1933

As a result of a wager, Mr
Samson, who claims to be
the strongest man in the
world, holds together a pair
of shire horses at Croydon.
24th June, 1933

Cycle racing at Brooklands.
25th June, 1933

A contrast in clothing in the great heatwave of 1933: Children meet a Grenadier Guardsman on duty outside Buckingham Palace, London.

4th July, 1933

The Duchess of York playing
a game with children at
the opening ceremony of
the Boys and Girls Club at
Dagenham, Essex.
6th July, 1933

Jockey Gordon Richards relaxing with his wife and two sons at Shoreham-on-Sea. In this year Richards set a record by riding 12 consecutive winners, including all six at Chepstow.
24th July, 1933

The 'Barnstormers' playing
at The Barn Club.
1st September, 1933

A street scene on Archway
Road in North London.
16th September, 1933

A British Union of Fascists
bugler.
20th October, 1933

Bakers and chimney sweeps
at a carnival.
24th October, 1933

Record-holder E C
Fernihough on an Excelsior
JAP 175 c.c. motorcycle, at
the Brooklands race track.
31st October, 1933

Guards for the British Union of Fascists, outside its new London headquarters. The membership of the BUF grew from 10,000 at the beginning of 1933 to 50,000 in June of 1934.

1st December, 1933

John Cobb (L) with his
Napier Railton.
31st March, 1934

Manchester United
goalkeeper John Hacking (L)
claims the ball.
5th May, 1934

One of the Whitsun attractions at Hastings is a boxing ring constructed on a raft anchored near the shore. Classes of young girl boxers have been formed and displays attract much attention among holidaymakers.
20th May, 1934

Corporal Harrison, aged
75, playing a wood for the
Pensioners. London Warders
v Chelsea Pensioners.
11th June, 1934

The Duchess of York,
with Princess Elizabeth
and Princess Margaret,
arriving at Olympia for the
International Horse show.
26th June, 1934

Fred Perry lunges to play a
backhand at Wimbledon.
30th June, 1934

E Gordon-Simpson (L) and
Joan Richmond (R) before
the start of the racing at
Brooklands.
7th July, 1934

Aviation pioneer and aircraft designer Thomas Sopwith (R) and his wife at the wheel of his yacht 'Endeavour'.
7th July, 1934

Bognor Regis beach.
1st August, 1934

Camping scene at
Hoddesdon, Hertfordshire.
1st August, 1934

The Austin Radio Divan
set, comprising a radio set,
divan, bookcase, and electric
clock.
15th August, 1934

Thames Police headquarters
at Wapping.
7th September, 1934

Lowestoft fishermen
mending their nets.
8th September, 1934

Children play on a swing.
23rd October, 1934

A display of turkeys in a
butcher's during Christmas
shopping week.
19th December, 1934

The **1930s** Britain in Pictures

A man goes through
an automatic turnstile
at Stonehenge.
6th January, 1935

England's Peter Cranmer
(second R) outstrips
Ireland's David Lane (R)
after receiving a pass from
teammate Bus Leyland (L).
9th February, 1935

A factory at St John's Wood is busily transforming lumps of willow into bats. The picture shows a huge stack of shaped willows at the factory ready to be manufactured into cricket bats for the coming season.
27th March, 1935

The 3rd Coldstream Guards chair their captain, holding the cup, as they celebrate their 2-1 victory over the Guards Depot in the Household Brigade Senior Cup final.
2nd April, 1935

(L-R) Miss Isabella Rieben, Miss Cradock-Hartopp, Lady Alness, Mrs P Ceron and England captain Miss Phyllis Wade at the Ladies' Golf Union International Meeting at Ranelagh Club, Barnes.
10th April, 1935

Victor Stafford's
streamlined car.
10th April, 1935

Miss Ida Santarelli
and her orchestra.
16th April, 1935

Fire crews in asbestos suits walking in the flames during a fire-fighting demonstration at an airfield.
16th April, 1935

An Austin 7 taxi cab
in London.
1st May, 1935

The orthoptoscope
apparatus to cure squints,
at Moorfields Eye Hospital
in London.
12th May, 1935

A scene from George
Bernard Shaw's play
'The Simpleton of
the Unexpected Isle'.
20th May, 1935

The top three drivers and their cars after the British Empire Trophy race, with winner Freddy Dixon (R, in car 32) celebrating with a glass of champagne.
6th July, 1935

Two of the competitors
during their bout in the
shadow of old Lincoln's Inn.
Epee Championships,
semi finals.
12th July, 1935

Dogs being bathed.
23rd July, 1935

Facing page: Holiday
crowds at Waterloo Station
in London.
23rd July, 1935

Irish Guards bandsmen
at the newly re-named
Waterloo Eastern Station.
23rd July, 1935

Facing page:
A country scene.
1935

An open air café
with attendants.
1935

A 'notificator' machine where messages can be written and left at Liverpool Street Station in London.
21st August, 1935

An ice cream seller.
26th August, 1935

Busmen from the Green
Line Windsor Bus service
on strike.
1st September, 1935

The SS 'Albertville', a steam passenger-freighter, moored in the Thames.
6th September, 1935

A scene from 'Hiawatha' at
the Royal Albert Hall.
6th September, 1935

A soldier from the Seaforth Highlanders using a Hotchkiss machine gun during army manoeuvres.
7th September, 1935

A mobile field kitchen of the
Welsh Guards Regiment.
7th September, 1935

St George's Hospital,
London.
26th September, 1935

Facing page: Crowds waiting
for buses at London Bridge.
26th September, 1935

Children playing at
Greenwich riverside.
26th September, 1935

British music hall composer
and star Harry Champion
poses for a picture.
25th October, 1935

A market scene at Crisp
Street in Poplar, London.
11th November, 1935

Feeding herons in St. James's Park, London.
11th November, 1935

An 'Ole Bill Bus' (an LGOC B-43 type bus) taking part in the Lord Mayor's Show parade. These buses were used during the First World War by the British Army to transport troops to the front, as mobile command posts and general service and eventually to take many of them home from the front once the war had ended.

11th November, 1935

Two ladies astride an 1895
Crank Drive Motorcycle (R)
and a 500 New Imperial
Twin (L).
29th November, 1935

The Emperor of Abyssinia
(Ethiopia), Haile Selassie,
is presented with a bouquet
of flowers during a visit to
Great Britain.
1936

Motorcycles parked
outside Wembley.
1936

Staff from John Sanders Ltd
line the railway embankment
to pay their last respects to
King George V as his body
is transported to Windsor on
a GWR train.

23rd January, 1936

Recruits to the Army parade
at Scotland Yard.
29th January, 1936

Bristol Bulldog single seat
biplane fighter aircraft lined
up for take-off.
1st March, 1936

Champion steel-bender
George Challard trains
his four year old son in
the art of strongmanship
by standing on his chest
to toughen him up.
27th March, 1936

Umbrellas in the lost
property department at
Waterloo Station, London.
1st April, 1936

The Royal Mail Ship
(RMS) 'Queen Mary'.
22nd April, 1936

Pith helmets at Waterloo
Station lost property office.
5th May, 1936

Teacher and children in a classroom in St Bride and Bridewell Precinct School.
6th May, 1936

An elephant playing a
mouth-organ at Whipsnade
Safari Park.
15th May, 1936

Cunard-White Star Liner
'Queen Mary' leaves
Southampton on her maiden
voyage to New York, USA.
27th May, 1936

A fashionable woman
attends the Ascot races.
15th June, 1936

Autocycles on Hammersmith
Bridge, London.
16th June, 1936

Peter Ward breaks the tape to win the three miles in an English Native record time of 14 minutes 15.8 seconds.
11th July, 1936

King Edward VIII escaped
attack when a man
(known as George Andrew
McMahon, real name
Jerome Bannigan, a fascist
sympathiser) in the crowd
near Wellington Arch,
London, produced a revolver.
16th July, 1936

A policeman holding up
traffic in Fleet Street.
24th July, 1936

A telegraph linesman
at work on a pole.
24th July, 1936

Two farm wagons loaded
with hay passing through
the River Wye.
1st August, 1936

A London Transport trolley bus at Crayford in south east London.
1st August, 1936

People dressed up with
comedy costumes and
heads at Southend Carnival.
7th August, 1936

Facing page: Filming on set
at Denham Studios.
7th August, 1936

A wrecked bicycle after a
crash involving a bus.
4th September, 1936

A group of accordion players
outside Central Hall, London.
1st October, 1936

Loading luxury motor cars onto the liner 'Queen Mary' at Southampton.
13th October, 1936

Sugar beet being unloaded
at Halstead, Essex.
13th October, 1936

Policemen arrest a protestor
during a demonstration by
the unemployed.
14th October, 1936

The Baird Control room
at the Alexandra Palace
Television Station in North
London.
25th October, 1936

A miniature 'Brooklands' racetrack, on the promenade at the foot of Brighton's Regency Square.
10th November, 1936

Facing page: The Jarrow marchers pass through Lavendon on their way to protest in London over unemployment.
26th October, 1936

The ruins of the Crystal
Palace, London, after it was
burned down.
30th November, 1936

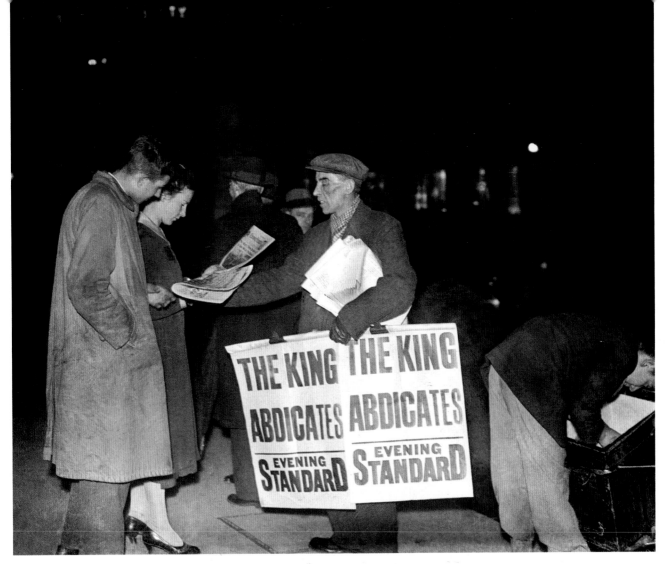

Selling newspapers at
Ludgate Circus when King
Edward VIII abdicated.
10th December, 1936

Street musicians dressed
as Father Christmas.
1st December, 1936

A hawker selling toys on
a kerbstone at Holborn.
4th January, 1937

The Embankment from
Hungerford Bridge showing
the 'Shell House'.
1st February, 1937

Telegraph messengers in old
(L) and new uniforms.
1st February, 1937

Chorus girls practising tap
dancing with choreographer
Buddy Bradley.
1st February, 1937

Chorus girls in the dressing
room of a London theatre.
1st February, 1937

Bells being cast at Croydon.
15th March, 1937

Dancer Margaret Morris
rehearsing the 'White Lotus'
dance.
15th March, 1937

Beecher's Brook second
time around showing the
winner 'Royal Mail' leading
the field, ahead of 'Flying
Minute' and 'Delachance',
during the Grand National
at Aintree.
24th March, 1937

The Duke and Duchess
of York arriving with their
daughters Elizabeth aged 11,
and Margaret (R) at Central
Hall, Westminster, for
the Coronation concert
for children.
6th April, 1937

Tommy Farr, British Empire
Heavyweight Champion.
6th April, 1937

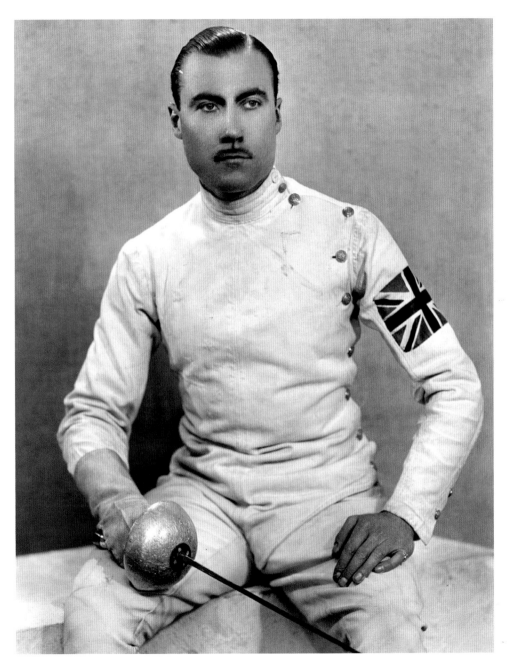

Fencer, Charles
de Beaumont.
8th April, 1937

Sunderland captain Raich
Carter (R) receives the FA
Cup from the Queen (C).
1st May, 1937

Facing page: Cliff Bastin (R)
of Arsenal tries a flying shot
against Bolton at Highbury
Stadium.
1st May, 1937

Queen Elizabeth with her husband King George VI and their daughters, Princess Elizabeth and Princess Margaret. The picture was taken after the Coronation.
12 May, 1937

F Charles, L Van Praeg
and J Ornston at the first
speedway test of 1937
at Wembley.
24th May, 1937

Schoolboys run from
the playground at the end
of term.
15th June, 1937

Facing page: The
SS 'Aquitania' and
the SS 'Berengaria' at
Southampton Docks.
5th July, 1937

John Cobb in his Napier
Railton at speed during
the 500 miles Race at
Brooklands.
18th September, 1937

The 'Radio Queen',
Miss Elmira Humphreys.
22nd September, 1937

A steam train and a
streamlined diesel Leyland
railway engine.
26th October, 1937

Rugby player Prince Alex
Obolensky (R) dives to make
a tackle.
5th November, 1937

An elephant pushing a child
on a toy horse.
7th December, 1937

Facing page: Potential
recruits enlist at the first of
10 mobile recruiting offices
on duty outside Victory
House in Kingsway, London,
during the period in which
Britain prepared herself for
the outbreak of the Second
World War.
1938

A warning is given to
motorists in a manoeuvre
area by a military cyclist
riding ahead of troops.
1938

A farm hand with some specimens after picking the tobacco harvest at the farm of A J Bandon at Church Crookham.
1938

Demolishing the rear of
Whitehall for rebuilding.
1938

Soldiers wearing gas masks
during an air raid drill in
a shelter.
4th February, 1938

An ant-aircraft gun on
display outside a Territorial
recruiting bureau at Mansion
House, London.
4th February, 1938

For the second year in succession, Miss L Styles won the Southern Counties Ladies' Cross-Country Run over a course of three miles. The picture shows the unusual start of the race at Hounslow when the competitors broke through the tapes placed at the starting point.

19th February, 1938

Sandbag dummies for parachute drops being loaded on a Vickers Virginia aeroplane at Hendon Aerodrome.
28th February, 1938

Miss Tania Sharman,
a television star, displaying
a new Cossor television set.
19th March, 1938

Henry Davis broadcasting
dance music from
Hammersmith Palais.
5th April, 1938

King George VI and Queen
Elizabeth leaving the
Government building after
HRH had opened the Empire
Exhibition in Scotland, from
a dais in the Ibrox Stadium
in Glasgow.
4th May, 1938

Female members of the
Auxilliary Fire Service
knitting, complete with steel
helmets.
1st June, 1938

Bunny Austin (L) shakes hands with Khe Sin Kie (R) after beating him in the final of the London Lawn Tennis Championships at Queen's Club.

18th June, 1938

Crowds queuing outside
Lord's on Saturday morning
to see the continuation of the
Wally Hammond/Les Ames
fourth wicket partnership
in the Test match between
England and Australia.
25th June, 1938

The bootblack
at Charing Cross.
12th July, 1938

Workmen in a joiners'
shop making furniture at
Cammell Lairds shipyard in
Birkenhead.
10th August, 1938

Facing page: Vickers
Wellington bombers flying
in close formation in clouds.
10th August, 1938

Mrs A C Lace signals
in the pits at Brooklands.
29th August, 1938

British Prime Minister Neville Chamberlain waves his hat as he boards an aircraft bound for Munich, where he is to have talks with the German Fuhrer, Adolf Hitler, over the future of the disputed Czech Sudetenland.
28th September, 1938

Birmingham's Fred Harris (R)
hits the ball past Charlton
Athletic goalkeeper Sam
Bartram.
1st October, 1938

The Women's Billiard
Championship has
commenced at Burroughs'
Hall in Soho Square,
London. Picture shows
Mrs McDougall of London,
the champion, making
a shot watched by her
opponent, Mrs G Holman,
also of London.
7th November, 1938

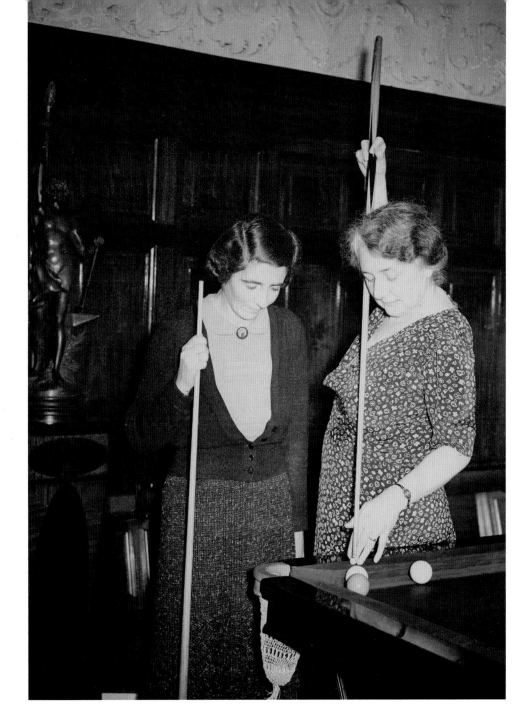

A snowball fight in Trafalgar
Square, London.
7th November, 1938

A new leap start autogiro for
the RAF and Navy.
10th January, 1939

Women members of the
League of Health & Beauty
performing exercises.
10th January, 1939

Princess Margaret observes the pantomime performance of 'Red Riding Hood' at the Royal Opera House, Covent Garden.

3rd February, 1939

(L-R) Wales' Wilf Wooller
(L) dodges a tackle from
Scotland's John Craig (R)
during a rugby Five Nations
Championship match.
4th February, 1939

Dick Seaman and his wife
Erica show off some of the
magnificent trophies he has
collected for his motor racing
exploits.
17th March, 1939

Sir Thomas Beecham with
his symphony orchestra.
10th April, 1939

Winston Churchill addresses
a recruiting meeting at the
Mansion House, London,
during the European crisis
(the build-up to the outbreak
of the Second World War).
24th April, 1939

Portsmouth captain Jimmy
Guthrie holds the FA Cup
aloft as he is chaired by his
teammates.
29th April, 1939

No19 Fighter Squadron, based at Duxford, Cambs, flying their Spitfire aircraft in formation in the year of the outbreak of the Second World War. No19 was the first RAF Squadron to be equipped with the new Supermarine Spitfire, the only fighter aircraft to be used throughout the entire War.

1st May, 1939

Vickers Wellington bombers
on RAF exercises.
1st May, 1939

Piccadilly Circus, London.
1st May, 1939

Formations of Vickers Wellington bombers fly over one of the aircraft on the ground, during an airshow.
6th May, 1939

Alex Kyle, winner of the 1939
British Amateur Open Golf
Championship.
17th May, 1939

A woman delivers milk,
with her gas mask.
7th July, 1939

The start of the Soap-Box
Derby at Brooklands.
16th July, 1939

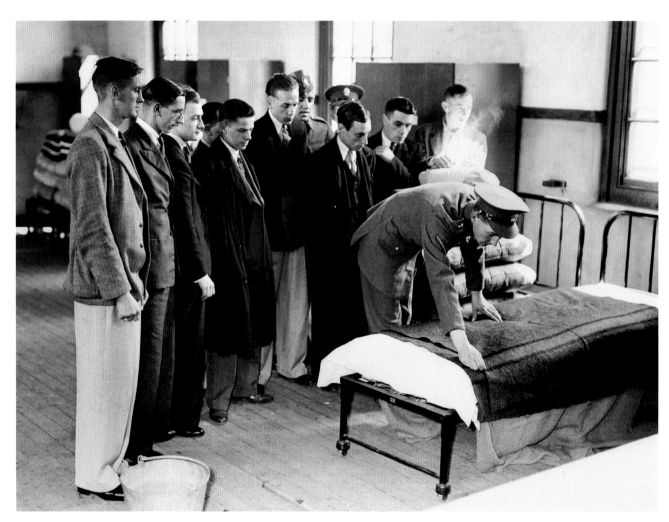

New recruits for the British
Territorial Army being shown
how to make a bed.
24th July, 1939

Women on their way to work
with gas masks in boxes.
1st August, 1939

Children being evacuated.
1st September, 1939

Facing page: London schoolboys, complete with gas masks in cardboard boxes and luggage, all set for evacuation to the country.
1st September, 1939

Filling sandbags in London.
1st September, 1939

London evacuees.
1st September, 1939

A steel-helmeted policeman
on duty at the Bank traffic
intersection in London.
2nd September, 1939

Women ambulance drivers
have a dance.
12th September, 1939

A milk bar sandbagged
as an air raid shelter.
12th September, 1939

The Guards' band marching
in service dress.
12th September, 1939

A female garage attendant.
12th September, 1939

Billy Cotton with his band.
12th September, 1939

Woman painting a keyhole
with luminous paint for
the blackout.
4th October, 1939

Evacuated children
having their dinner.
4th October, 1939

British troops attend an
ENSA (Entertainments
National Service
Association) show.
8th October, 1939

Soldiers peeling potatoes.
10th October, 1939

BLACKOUT TIME TO-NIGHT IS AT

An air-raid warden sets a black-out time clock indicator at an A.R.P. post near London.
1st November, 1939

Facing page: Christmas parcels being sorted at Mount Pleasant.
7th November, 1939

London General Omnibus
Company busmen civil
air guards on parade with
Dawson Paul, the instructor.
15th December, 1939

Public school cadets
inspect RAF Spitfires.
15th December, 1939

A jitterbug competition
in progress.
16th December, 1939

Cabaret girls at
the Paradise Club.
16th December, 1939

The Publishers gratefully acknowledge PA Photos, from whose extensive archive the photographs in this book have been selected. Personal copies of the photographs in this book, and many others, may be ordered online at www.prints.paphotos.com

For more information, please contact:

Ammonite Press

AE Publications Ltd. 166 High Street, Lewes, East Sussex, BN7 1XU, United Kingdom

Tel: 01273 488005 Fax: 01273 402866

www.ae-publications.com